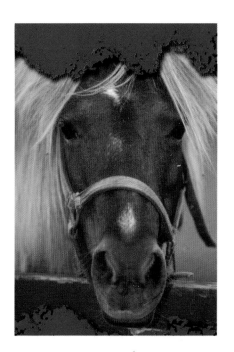

Animals

Dona Herweck Rice

Table of Contents

Mammals   4

Reptiles   8

Birds   12

Glossary   16

There are many kinds of
animals. How many do
you know?

Mammals

Mammals have fur. A bear is furry.

Mammals get warm from inside their bodies. A cat is very warm.

Mammals come in many
sizes. A hamster is small.

An elephant is a large
mammal.

Most reptiles lay eggs.
Crocodiles bury their
eggs to keep them safe.

Reptiles get heat from
outside their bodies. A
snake uses the sun to get
warm.

Many reptiles have scales.
A lizard has scaly skin.

Some reptiles have shells.
A turtle has a hard shell to
hide inside.

Birds

Birds have wings and feathers. An eagle has very large wings.

Birds lay eggs. A mother robin sits in her nest to take care of her eggs.

Most birds can fly, but
turkeys raised on farms
can not.

Some birds are very colorful.
A parrot is a beautiful bird
with many colors.

Glossary

 bear

 lizard

 cat

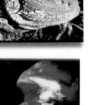 parrot

 crocodile

 robin

 eagle

 snake

 elephant

 turkey

 hamster

 turtle